GO GREEN!

Written by
Liz Gogerly

Illustrated by
Miguel Sanchez

W
FRANKLIN WATTS
LONDON · SYDNEY

Franklin Watts

First published in Great Britain in 2018
by The Watts Publishing Group
© The Watts Publishing Group 2018

Managing editor: Victoria Brooker
Design: Anthony Hannant (Little Red Ant)

ISBN: 978 1 4451 5849 5 (hbk)
ISBN: 978 1 4451 5850 1 (pbk)

Printed in China

Franklin Watts
An imprint of Hachette Children's Group
Part of The Watts Publishing Group
Carmelite House
50 Victoria Embankment
London EC4Y 0DZ
An Hachette UK Company

www.hachette.co.uk
www.franklinwatts.co.uk

MIX
Paper from
responsible sources
FSC® C104740

Contents

The Birthday Party

The children have had a great time at Anjali's birthday party. They played party games like pass the parcel and musical statues and there were loads of great prizes. Afterwards they had a balloon fight.

The party food was delicious, with plenty of chocolate for everyone. And, Anjali loved unwrapping all her presents. All in all, it was really great fun but now there's a HUGE mess! And that has made the children stop and think ...

Great present but so much rubbish!

What a mess!

▲ Fred the Ted
This teddy bear is a great gift today but what will happen to him in the future? Follow his journey through the book.

Plastic toys ▲
Plastic toys cannot be recycled and usually end up in landfill or polluting our oceans. Cheap plastic figures won as prizes at a party are not made from the kind of plastic that will ever biodegrade.

4

▲ Balloons

Balloons can be great fun at a party but never let them go outside. They eventually return to land or into the sea. Many animals, birds and fish mistake them for food and this can kill them. Most balloons are not easily biodegradable and last for years.

We left loads of food.

What happens to all the rubbish?

Food waste ▲

Did you know that about one third of food that is produced in the world for humans to eat is wasted. All that food we throw away could be used to feed other people. Also, if we didn't waste so much, we could cut back on the resources we need to produce our food such as energy, water and land.

5

What Happens to Rubbish?

Anjali's party was just the beginning for these children. Next, they wanted to know what happened to those sacks filled with food and paper plates. Noah told them about a book from school where it said that our rubbish is taken away to landfill sites. These are big holes in the ground where our waste is tipped.

Many households mix household waste with recyclable materials. All of this counts as household waste and it will go to landfill or be incinerated.

Black bin bags
Some plastic refuse sacks can take up to 1,000 years to degrade. We can buy degradable refuse bags that break down fully and harmlessly.

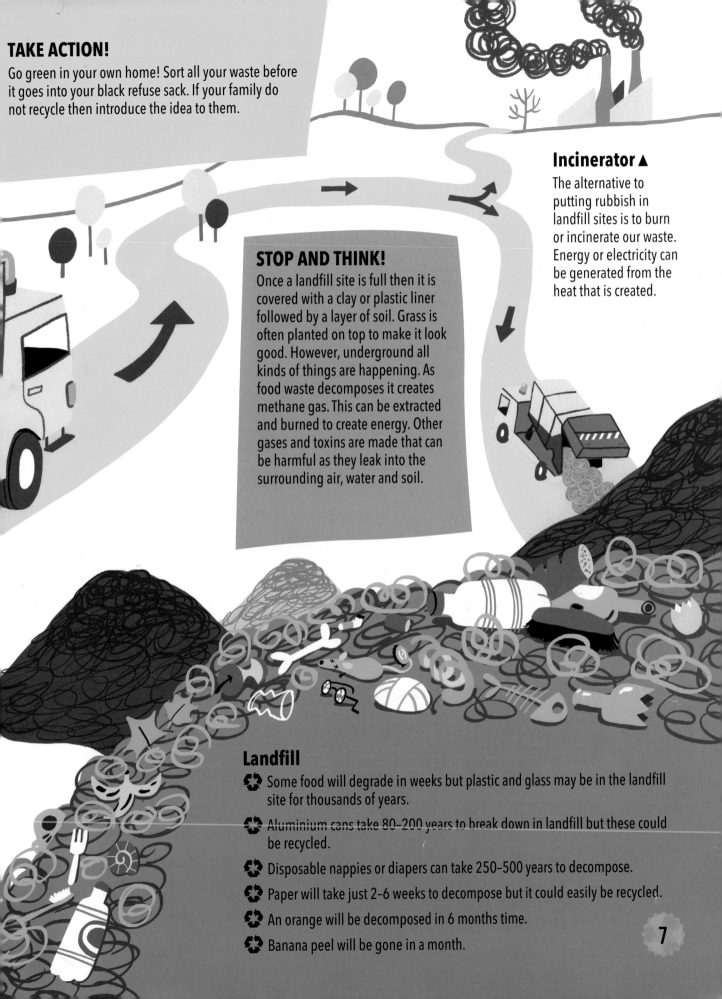

TAKE ACTION!

Go green in your own home! Sort all your waste before it goes into your black refuse sack. If your family do not recycle then introduce the idea to them.

Incinerator ▲

The alternative to putting rubbish in landfill sites is to burn or incinerate our waste. Energy or electricity can be generated from the heat that is created.

STOP AND THINK!

Once a landfill site is full then it is covered with a clay or plastic liner followed by a layer of soil. Grass is often planted on top to make it look good. However, underground all kinds of things are happening. As food waste decomposes it creates methane gas. This can be extracted and burned to create energy. Other gases and toxins are made that can be harmful as they leak into the surrounding air, water and soil.

Landfill

✿ Some food will degrade in weeks but plastic and glass may be in the landfill site for thousands of years.

✿ Aluminium cans take 80–200 years to break down in landfill but these could be recycled.

✿ Disposable nappies or diapers can take 250–500 years to decompose.

✿ Paper will take just 2–6 weeks to decompose but it could easily be recycled.

✿ An orange will be decomposed in 6 months time.

✿ Banana peel will be gone in a month.

Go Green in the Countryside

The children think of more examples of how people do not dispose of their waste properly. Mason remembers when he went to a festival in the countryside. His family arrived early and they pitched their tent in a field. Everything was so green and beautiful. More people arrived with all their camping gear and boxes of food and drink. The festival lasted two days. Everyone had a brilliant time but afterwards the field was a HUGE mess …

The four 'r's

A festival can be clean, green fun if we remember to **r**educe, **r**euse, **r**ecycle and take **r**esponsibility.

Wow, I love the countryside.

TAKE ACTION!

Protecting the natural environment and not harming animals, birds, plants or trees is important. Most countries have a countryside code. This is a list of rules you should follow when you visit the countryside. Number one is to leave no trace of your visit and take all your litter home.

STOP AND THINK!
Estimated time for everyday items to decompose:
glass bottles: 1–2 million years
leather shoes: 25–40 years
rubber wellington boots: 50–80 years
nylon or synthetic fibres used in tents: 30–40 years.

After the festival ...

What have we done?

The fifth 'r' is respect
Everyone can enjoy the festival if we remember to respect the creatures around us. If you trample on the plants and flowers then some animals and insects lose their natural habitat.

Love Our Planet

Have you ever experienced 'a wake-up moment' about the environment like these children? Did you suddenly realise that the everyday things that you do have an impact on the world? Anjali, Noah, Lulu and Mason decide they want to take more responsibility and look after the planet. But why is it important to take action now?

Our oceans

Things we throw away without thinking contribute to a great waste island floating in our oceans. This drifting pile of rubbish is believed to be the size of India, Mexico and Europe combined. Much of this trash is plastic that will not decompose. Plastic waste, including plastic bags, is killing around 1 million sea creatures every year.

Global warming

Our planet is getting gradually hotter. This is called global warming. It is caused by carbon dioxide in the Earth's atmosphere. Many scientists believe we must cut carbon dioxide emissions (the gas that is produced) to slow down global warming. These emissions mostly come from burning fuel to create energy - such as when we use petrol to run cars or burn coal to create electricity or make heat.

More than 1 million species have become extinct because of global warming.

TAKE ACTION!

A simple eco-friendly thing to start doing is to walk or ride your bicycle to school. This cuts fuel usage which means less carbon dioxide emissions and pollution. And, it's healthier for you too.

Our rivers

Many of us are lucky enough to have clean running water in our homes. By 2025, according to USAID (the United States Agency for International Development), one third of the world's population will have water shortages. This is because of global warming, which causes climate change, and pollution.

STOP AND THINK!

Planet Earth is home to about 7.5 billion people. All of us rely upon this amazing planet for the air we breath, the water we drink and the food we eat. We also get to enjoy its countryside and oceans. Modern humans evolved 200,000 years ago. in all that time, the Earth has sustained us but now it is time for us to look after the planet ...

Time to 'Go Green'!

The children start making changes in their life. The next day, they ride their bikes to school rather than go by car. At school, they ask their teacher how they can do more to help the environment.

▼ Empty milk and juice containers are brought from home and reused as plant pots for seeds or water containers.

▼ This school gets environmentally-friendly stationery whenever it can. This paper is 100 per cent recycled.

This is a zero waste classroom. Recycling bins have been set up for paper, plastic and glass so nothing goes to landfill.

Paper isn't wasted here. It is reused to make new notebooks or cut up as scrap paper.
▲ Everyone writes on both sides too.

Pens and other bits of stationery are used until they wear out. They may not look shiny and new but they do the job just as well.

Ms Monroe is happy the children have decided to 'Go Green'! She explains that going green is about discovering how the planet is changing and what we can do about it. It's also about being environmentally friendly and making choices in our lives that help protect the planet. Ms Monroe has already made changes in her classroom to look after the environment.

▲ The children love to plant seeds and watch them grow. It's healthy to bring the outdoors into the classroom and it reminds the children how amazing nature can be.

STOP AND THINK!
Some plastics used in drink containers or bottles are biodegradable, which means that they will eventually break down or decompose. However, even these plastics can take between 450 to 1,000 years to break down completely and are harmful to the environment.

Reducing Carbon Emissions

Going green means understanding more about what is happening to our Earth and why it's a problem. Global warming, climate change and pollution are major challenges facing the world today.

Nobody knows for sure why the world is getting warmer but most scientists believe it is because of greenhouse gases like carbon dioxide. Carbon dioxide is emitted when we burn fossil fuels to create energy.

It's the simple everyday things that we all do that add to carbon emissions – whether that's warming our homes, cleaning our clothes, cooking our meals or driving our cars. The good news is that by going green we can reduce our carbon emissions.

Many of the activities that produce carbon dioxide are responsible for pollution too. If we can find ways to reduce carbon dioxide emissions then we can really help the environment.

To reduce our carbon emissions we need to think about the everyday things we do and find alternatives or make changes. To do this we need to look closely at the transport we use, the energy supply to our home, the energy use in our home, the food we eat and how we already reduce, reuse and recycle.

TAKE ACTION!

Decisions like walking or cycling to school rather than going by car will reduce your carbon emissions. If your home is powered by solar energy (power from the sun) you can reduce your emissions. Even switching off lights when you don't need them, or deciding to reuse and recycle, will reduce the energy you use.

Climate Change

Every small change we make to our lifestyle helps to reduce our carbon emissions which slows down climate change. But, why is climate change such a big deal?

Ms Monroe explains that the Earth is warming up very slowly. Since 1900 it has got about 0.8°C warmer. Some scientists think that by the end of the 21st century it could be warmer by about 2–5°C.

Extreme weather alert

Many experts agree that hotter temperatures will create different weather patterns. Some experts believe that extreme weather like heatwaves, droughts, storms and flooding will get worse as the planet heats up.

Extreme weather is becoming more frequent!

Nobody knows for sure how hot it will get.

TAKE ACTION!

Make your own climate! Small changes at home like turning down the heat can reduce your carbon emissions. Put on a jumper when you feel cold or move around. And, when it's hot don't switch on the air conditioning or an electric fan. Dress for the heat by wearing lighter, whiter clothes and seek the shade.

People and animals will lose their homes.

STOP AND THINK!
Climate change is affecting the lives of endangered animals. Polar bears in the Arctic depend on sea ice because it's where they live and hunt for food. The temperature in the Arctic is rising and the ice is melting - perhaps by about 4 per cent each decade. Life for polar bears will get more difficult as the ice recedes and scientists fear they could become extinct.

Flood warning!
Climate change is causing polar ice to melt and sea levels to rise. In the future this could cause flooding of coastal regions and the loss of low lying land.

Why Should We Reduce?

It's important that we reduce, reuse, recycle. The children want to know why it's so important to reduce waste. Luckily, their head teacher is already environmentally friendly and she explains the facts to them.

Money! It costs a lots of money, energy and natural resources to make everything – whether that's food or everyday items like the clothes we wear or the devices we use.

Transport! Transporting food and everything we need to live our lives costs money and because we still use mainly fossil fuels like petrol for transportation there is pollution too.

TAKE ACTION!

Borrow books from the library or from a friend. Rent a film digitally or buy a DVD from a charity shop. Try to buy durable items that will last so you don't end up throwing things away that end up in landfill.

STOP AND THINK!

Reducing the things we buy is the first important step you can take when you go green. Get into the habit of asking yourself if you need something before you buy it. At school there are often crazes for exciting new things – loom bands and spinner fidgets are two recent examples. But these things quickly go out of fashion and these objects cannot be recycled so they inevitably end up in landfill – do you really want to add to the waste mountain?

Waste! When we've finished with things, or it's become waste, then it costs money to get rid of it. Whether that's paying for the bin lorries that visit our streets to empty our rubbish bins or the incineration process to get rid of it.

Landfill! If our waste goes to a landfill site that causes problems too – dangerous toxins can leak into the surrounding area.

Pollution! Toxic landfill can kill animals and plants, and get into our water supply.

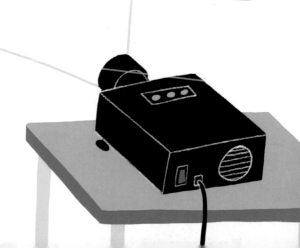

Why Do We Reuse?

To help the children understand why we should reuse things the school asked Ed from the local 'Reuse Superstore' to tell the children about his job.

Ed is an expert in giving things a 'second life'. People donate all kinds of things to his superstore – from furniture to white goods, such as fridges, to toys such as teddies. Ed makes sure that everything is used again, rather than taken to landfill sites. Most of us throw away things that other people need.

One person's trash is another person's treasure!

STOP AND THINK!

Lots of used, second-hand or pre-owned clothes that are rejected by charity shops in Europe and the USA are sent to developing nations. These clothes may not be fashionable but they are in great condition and there is a flourishing market for them in some places.

Refrigerator dilemmas

Refrigerators have a chemical called refrigerant inside which keeps things cool. Refrigerants are greenhouse gases so they are bad for the environment. For this reason all fridges and freezers should not be thrown away or put in landfill.

Sofa solutions

Bulky waste like sofas take up a lot of space in landfill. As long as a sofa has a label with fire regulations on it then it can be re-used by another family, otherwise it must be thrown away.

Reuse fridges

As it's so difficult to recycle or dispose of our old fridges it makes sense that we find new homes for the ones that are still working or can be fixed.

SMIDGE

Hard recycling

White goods like refrigerators, washing machines and ovens are difficult to recycle. They are bulky, heavy and have to be dismantled carefully to recycle the steel, copper and aluminium within.

Reuse in Action

The children are inspired by the idea of reusing things. At home they look for things they don't want anymore and find clothes, books, toys and sports equipment that could be given away. They want to know if there is a way they can swap or exchange these things for what they do need.

Lulu discovers loads of websites where it is easy to swap almost anything. There are also plenty of online sites where you can give your stuff away or get things – for free!

STOP AND THINK!

The Freecycle organisation began in Tucson, Arizona in the USA in 2003. The idea was to give away unwanted reusable goods to reduce waste and to prevent so much going to landfill in the desert. The items were OFFERED online and the giver decided who RECEIVED an item from the posts they received. People could also post the things they WANTED and let the group know when they had RECEIVED what they wanted. Today there are about 7 million members of Freecycle groups in around 121 countries all over the world. The rules are simple: everything that is advertised must be free.

TAKE ACTION!

Encourage your family to join up to a local organisation like Freecycle and see what you can stop going to landfill. Everything you give away or receive reduces waste and helps to reduce your carbon footprint.

Why Do We Recycle?

Recycling is important too if you want to go green. Recycling is the third 'R' for a reason though – it takes more money, more energy and more resources to recycle something.

To find out more the children visit a material recovery facility (MRF) where a woman called Ava tells them how they sort the recycled products. At this centre the recyclable rubbish arrives mixed together ...

STOP AND THINK!

By recycling one tonne of fizzy drink cans we can stop three tonnes of carbon dioxide emissions.

TAKE ACTION!

Become the recycle chief in your household. Take batteries to separate banks – many supermarkets have used battery banks inside. Tetrapaks or drinks containers as well as textiles are often collected separately. Discover what else is being recycled in your area and get to it!

GLASS   PLASTIC   TEXTILES

1. The mixed recycling is tipped onto a conveyor belt. The materials are hand checked for recyclable glass, plastic bags and textiles – these will be processed separately.

2. Now the recycled waste is separated out into different materials. The spinning action inside this big drum, called the 'trommel', will separate items like cans and plastic bottles.

3. Compressed jets of air, from this machine nicknamed the 'air knife', separate out the paper.

4. A massive magnet draws steel cans out of the mix and electromagnetics repel the aluminium cans so they can be separated out.

5. Infrared cameras scan the bottles to find which type of plastic they are made from. Jets of air remove the various kinds of plastic to different areas.

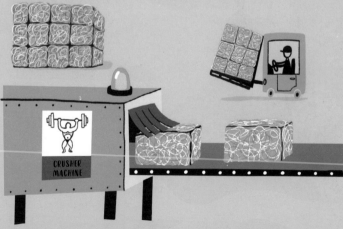

CRUSHER MACHINE

6. A giant crusher compacts the separated materials into large bales. The large bales of separated material are sold to companies that will make new 'earth-friendly' products or use them again in industry.

The Recycle Cycle

Once the items have been sorted the children discover what happens next in the recycling process.

BEFORE:

Cardboard

Paper

Glass bottles

Aluminium cans

Batteries

Steel cans and aerosols

AFTER:

Cardboard tubes and packing

Other paper products

New glass products

New cans, signs or seating

Base metals and plastic

Steel sheets used in construction, car and packaging industries

The children look to see what their items could become once recycled. Old paper can easily be recycled and used again. Even tired old clothes can be used as filling for bedding. The children are amazed at the possibilities ...

BEFORE:

AFTER:

Cooking oil

Biofuel for heating

Garden waste

Compost

Soft plastics

Backpacks, carpet and sleeping bags

Wood

Animal bedding

Textiles

Used to stuff bedding

Second Chance of Life

The children go in search of other ways that people are recycling materials to produce ethical and eco-friendly goods. The children find out that big companies are turning old trainers into soft and safe playground surfaces …

The new and exciting life cycle of a pair of trainers …

Most kids love trainers – especially when they're the latest 'must have' ones.

But every trainer has its day – either they get too small or they get a bit worn out.

You can give your old trainers to charity. Or, you can put them in recycling bins for shoes.

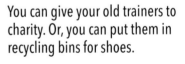

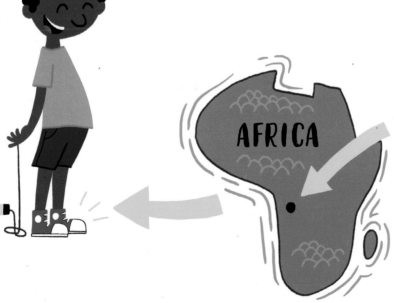

The shoes that go to recycling centres may be sent to children in less developed countries and distributed to children that need them.

Some trainers are being sent to factories where the rubber soles are ground down to make a new material called 'grind'.

Grind is used to surface pavements, playgrounds and running tracks.

STOP AND THINK!

You can recycle materials in your own home. Old crayons can be melted down to make new groovy crayons. Put the melted crayons into empty glue stick containers so you will be able to roll the crayons up and down.

TAKE ACTION!

Look out for other clothes that have been made from recycled materials. Plastic bottles make great hoodies but some inventive designers have made dresses from sweet wrappers, plastic bags, black bin bags and newspaper.

Make it Green

The idea of upcycling or reusing parts of things to make something else really appeals to the children. Their art teacher helps them to make some cool stuff at school. Reusing and recycling things that they would normally throw away feels good and is a great hobby.

The children make an awesome bowling set from old plastic bottles. Use your imagination and see what you have lying around to come up with a unique design.

STOP AND THINK!

Upcycling means reusing something in such a way that it is better than it was before. People mostly upcycle their rubbish or something they would have thrown away. A good example is old furniture. A lick of paint and a few new handles on a chest of drawers will give it a different look. Upcycling like this tends to be cheaper than buying new too.

MAKE AN AWESOME BOWLING SET!

What you need:

x 10

10 x plastic bottles of the same shape and size (or containers)

Paint, stickers, glitter or anything else you can find for decoration

PVA glue

Water or sand to fill the bottles

Ball

Instructions:

1) Clean the bottles and remove all the lids – put them in a safe place for later.

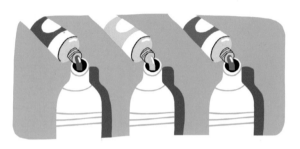

2) Squirt a different coloured paint into each bottle. If the paint is thick then add a little water to the paint.

3) Put the lids back on to the bottles and get ready to shake. Keep shaking until the paint coats the whole of the inside of each bottle.

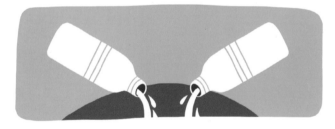

4) Remove the lids from the bottles and pour out any excess paint.

5) The decoration doesn't have to end there. Add ribbon or glitter to the outside. Paint faces or make interesting creatures out of each bottle. Let your bottles dry overnight.

6) Fill the bottles halfway with sand or water and put the lids back on securely. Your set is ready to go ...

Eco Action Outside

One day Sam from another local green organisation comes into school to talk about how they can be more environmentally friendly in the school playground. He is really impressed by everything they do already – especially the vegetable patch. He shows them how to make their own compost heap so they have good quality compost to use on their crops.

▲ These wildflowers really get things buzzing – they attract bees and other insects to the school gardens. Bumble bees are in decline and they need nectar from the flowers to survive. In return they pollinate the flowers and vegetables.

▲ Tyres can be recycled and used again on vehicles but they are great fun in a playground. The children at this school helped to design the tyre-inspired playground equipment.

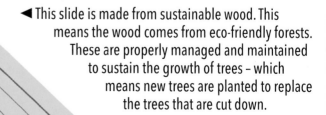

◀ This slide is made from sustainable wood. This means the wood comes from eco-friendly forests. These are properly managed and maintained to sustain the growth of trees – which means new trees are planted to replace the trees that are cut down.

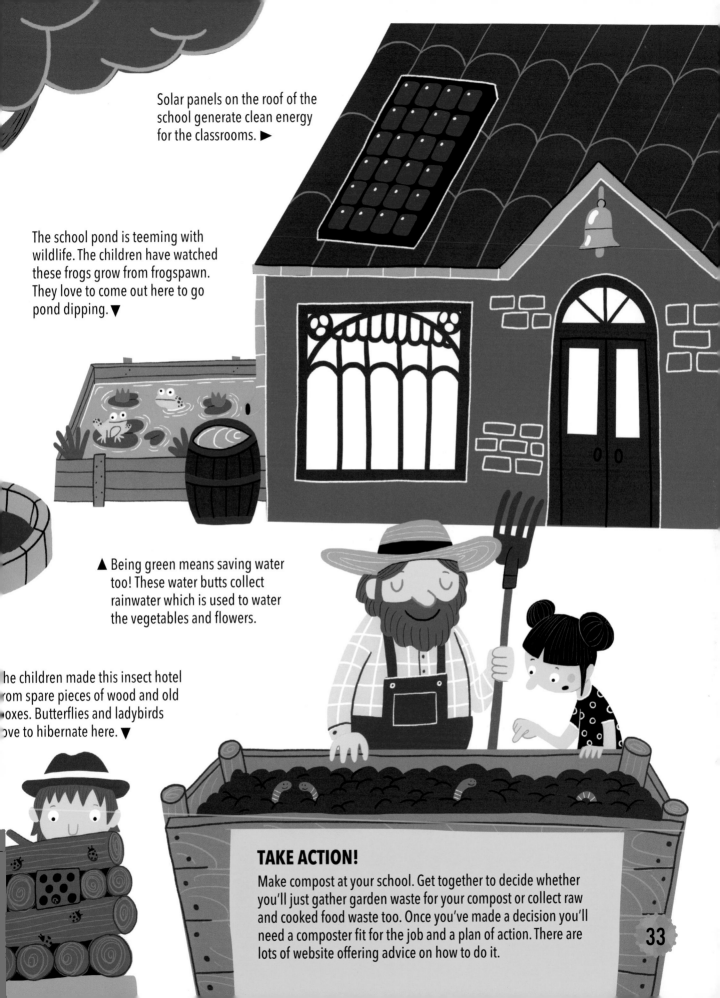

Solar panels on the roof of the school generate clean energy for the classrooms. ▶

The school pond is teeming with wildlife. The children have watched these frogs grow from frogspawn. They love to come out here to go pond dipping. ▼

▲ Being green means saving water too! These water butts collect rainwater which is used to water the vegetables and flowers.

he children made this insect hotel rom spare pieces of wood and old oxes. Butterflies and ladybirds ove to hibernate here. ▼

TAKE ACTION!

Make compost at your school. Get together to decide whether you'll just gather garden waste for your compost or collect raw and cooked food waste too. Once you've made a decision you'll need a composter fit for the job and a plan of action. There are lots of website offering advice on how to do it.

33

The School Dinner Challenge

The vegetables growing outside the classroom make the children think more about what they eat. And, making compost in the playground makes them consider food waste.

Mr Lee is the school cook and he thinks there are lots of ways to be eco-friendly in the kitchen. Home-cooked food using fresh ingredients is better for you and there is less packaging – this helps to reduce waste.

Food waste is a huge problem in school canteens. Good, tasty food is less likely to be left. Regular changes to the menu means nobody gets bored. Food waste bins in the kitchen ensure no food goes to landfill sites.

▼ Freshly baked cakes are yummy and don't have preservatives in them. Real fruit add sweetness and flavour.

Mr Lee tends to shop locally for food to reduce transportation.

MENU ♥

Mr Lee puts healthy food choices at the front of the counter. The children are in such a rush sometimes that they grab the first thing they see!

▲ There are lots of vegetables and salad in these school dinners.

WASTE

TAKE ACTION!

Next time you have a packed lunch or a picnic then aim for a zero-waste lunch. This means using reusable bottles and containers rather than drinks in plastic bottles or cartons of juice or pre-packaged foods. It also means reducing food waste – so make sure you gobble up everything or give it away to a friend. At school, you can compete with other classes to find out who can reduce their waste the most!

The Green Team at Home

Going green at school was a breeze but how was it at home?

Noah is on a mission at his home. He makes sure that all the lights are switched off in empty rooms and computers are turned off overnight. The washing is hung out to dry on the washing line rather than being put in the dryer.

Lulu's parents installed solar panels on the roof of their house last year. These generate enough electricity to power their home and there is even a little bit left over to put back into the national grid (the network of power stations and energy generators that supply electricity in a country).

STOP AND THINK!

The average home in the UK has 34 light bulbs and in the USA that rises to 45. By replacing old inefficient bulbs for energy-efficient bulbs households can reduce the electricity they use.

Traditionally homes have been powered by electricity made from coal, gas and oil (fossil fuels) which create greenhouse gases and cause pollution. Solar power is a clean alternative because no fuel is burned to create the energy – it just comes from the sun.

Anjali loves to shower rather than use the bath. If she's quick, it saves energy and it cuts down water use. The average bath uses about 88 litres. A typical shower flows at about 8 litres per minute.

So a five-minute shower uses half as much water as a bath. Anjali never lets the tap run when she cleans her teeth either.

Mason's family use eco-friendly cleaning products or natural products like white vinegar to clean the windows. These products are not tested on animals nor do they pollute the environment.

TAKE ACTION!

Watch out for 'phantom users'! These are appliances such as computers, television sets and microwave ovens that use power even when they are turned off. They may have digital displays or lights that draw power even when they are off. The only way to stop this is to switch them off at the mains.

Energy Matters!

Clean energy from the sun (solar power), water (hydropower and geothermal power) and wind are the answer to our future energy needs.

Lily from the local Friends of the Earth organisation shows the children the exciting ways people all around the world are making the change to clean energy.

Wind power

The UK is the leader in offshore wind power. Wind farms out at sea have tall wind turbines measuring about 220 m (720 feet) high, which generate 7 or 8 megawatts (MW) each.

Power from onshore wind farms in the USA and China are the cheapest forms of energy in the world.

Solar power

China leads the way in solar power production, followed by Germany.

In 2017 China opened the biggest solar park in the world. Longyangxia has round 4 million solar panels which can be seen from space! It will produce 850 MW of power – enough to supply around 200,000 homes.

Water power

Hydropower is the leading form of renewable energy in the world. It is produced by running water through turbines.

China, the USA, Brazil, Canada, India and Russia were top of the league for hydropower in 2015. Three Gorges Dam in China is the biggest hydropower project in the world.

Fossil fuels

The change to clean, renewable energy is slow and it is estimated that more than 66 per cent of the world's electricity is generated from fossil fuels like coal, oil and natural gas (non-renewable sources).

Coal-fired power stations emit carbon dioxide and pollutants like mercury, which is harmful to our health.

Water Warriors

Water is the big issue for Lulu. She worries about pollution of our waterways and oceans. And, she is concerned about water supplies to countries all around the world – constant, clean water is a right for everyone.

There are hundreds of organisations (most of them charities) and individuals helping to keep the waterways, oceans and water supplies of the world clean and green.

WaterAid

Every year 315,000 children under five die from drinking dirty water. WaterAid is an international charity working hard to keep water supplies clean and safe.

Teams of volunteers work with local people in Africa, India and other less-developed countries to improve the water supply and create more sanitary conditions.

Garbage patches

There are five giant garbage patches floating in our oceans. These enormous masses contain old fishing nets, plastic containers, large plastic debris and microplastics. The heart of the Pacific patch measures a possible 1 million km^2 (386,000 miles). Some of this plastic breaks down and is a serious risk to marine life.

Ocean cleanup

A young Dutch inventor called Boyan Slat has founded an organisation called the Ocean Cleanup to get rid of these dangerous garbage patches. He has invented a system to rid the seas of plastic.

STOP AND THINK!

Microbeads found in toothpaste, facial scrubs and other cosmetics are a serious risk to animals and our environment. The microbeads get into our rivers, lakes and oceans. The beads are eaten by plankton which is eaten by fish which in turn can be eaten by birds. Many organisations are campaigning for a worldwide ban on microbeads used in cosmetics.

Transport and Pollution

Changing the ways we get around and the transport we use can affect pollution in the atmosphere.

▲ Big cars or 4x4 cars have bigger engines and use more fuel. Diesel cars are another threat to the environment. When diesel is burned tiny harmful particles are emitted.

▲ Old cars or vintage cars use more fuel.

There are many ways that we can drive our cars in a responsible way. ▼

♻ Car share or combine journeys to cut back.

♻ Go slower - this is the single most important thing you can do.

♻ Cut out air conditioning.

♻ Join a car club - this is a great way of covering small journeys.

Cycling is free. The money you save could be used to buy equipment for your bike like panniers and luggage racks. Your savings can be spent on taxis when you really need it or towards hiring a car for your holiday. ▶

JOIN US AND GO GREEN...IN THE CITY!

Are buses a green option?

♻ Buses tend to run on diesel, which emits dangerous pollutants.

♻ Public transport is a good idea because one large vehicle carries more passengers and relieves congestion on the road.

♻ Electric buses are the way forward if we want a greener option for towns and cities.

◀ Most motorbikes use less fuel than cars so there are fewer emissions.

STOP AND THINK!

The good news is that the benefits from cycling or walking for two hours a day in a busy city are greater than the harm we do to our body because of breathing in traffic fumes. Get into walking! It's brilliant exercise and you see the world close up.

♻ Electric cars produce fewer greenhouse gases.

♻ These cars are 100 per cent eco-friendly to run because they don't add pollutants to the atmosphere.

♻ Electric cars are more expensive to buy but the running costs are cheaper.

The Big Eco Festival

The children have been on a massive learning journey and they plan their own Eco Festival at school. They raise funds for a local green group and a water charity in Africa. It's a day of clean, green activities with healthy food and recycled prizes. Who knew that zero waste and the three 'Rs' could be so much fun?

Lemonade

WIND POWER

Anjali has a stand selling mini windmills to promote the idea of wind power.

See Your Own CARBON FOOTPRINT

Noah has a 'calculate your own carbon footprint' stand.

Edible wall ▼

Tomato ▶

Lettuce ▲

TAKE ACTION!

Pupil power! Don't wait for teachers to introduce green projects at school. If you are passionate about the environment then join the school council and set up your own recycling schemes, start your vegetable plot or 'edible wall' (a vertical planter filled with fresh food like lettuce and tomatoes) or mastermind fund-raising events for solar panels or water schemes for Africa.

Bicycle Repairs

Mason has set up a bicycle repair stand.

WATERAiD

Lulu is raising money for the charity WaterAid.

STOP AND THINK!

A school teacher in New York boosted his pupil's attendance by getting them into growing plants in the classroom. The children's attendance in his class rose from 43 to 93 per cent because they wanted to be there to care for their plants.

Glossary

Biodegradable Describes a material that can be broken down or decomposed by bacteria or other living organisms.

Car club A group of people that club together to rent or hire from a pool of vehicles.

Carbon dioxide A colourless gas which is produced by all animals when they breathe out and by plants during photosynthesis. It is also created when materials that contain carbon, such as coal, are burned.

Charity An organisation which raises money for those in need.

Clean energy Energy that is created from renewable sources such as from sunlight, wind or water – also known as renewable energy.

Climate change The long-term changes in the Earth's weather patterns.

Decompose To decay or become rotten. Leaves and dead plant material decompose into soil.

Diesel A kind of fuel that is used in diesel vehicles.

Drought A long period of low rainfall which leads to a shortage of water.

Eco-friendly Describes something that does not harm the environment.

Emission A discharge of something such as a gas or fumes. Greenhouse gases are described as an emission.

Endangered Describes something that is in a dangerous situation. An endangered animal is at risk of becoming extinct or dying out as a species.

Ethical Something that is moral or right. Ethical products are usually green, organic, energy efficient or fair trade.

Extinct If a species of an animal has died out then that animal is described as extinct.

Fire regulations Rules about fire safety that must be followed.

Fossil fuel A natural fuel, such as coal, oil or gas, that was created long ago from the remains of living things.

Geothermal power Electricity produced using steam from hot water wells deep underground.

Global warming The rise in temperature of the Earth that is causing long-term climate change.

Greenhouse gases Gases in the Earth's atmosphere that trap radiation from the sun to create the 'greenhouse effect' and cause global warming.

Heatwave A long period of very hot weather.

Hydropower Electricity generated from turbines that are turned by the force of fast-moving water.

Incinerate To burn something to ash.

Incinerator A machine that burns waste material at a high temperature.

Infrared camera A camera that forms thermal images rather than ordinary cameras that create images from visible light. This means infrared cameras can be used in the dark.

Landfill site A place where waste or rubbish is disposed of in the ground.

Methane gas A natural gas that leaks from landfill sites as the rubbish decomposes. It can be used as a fuel but it is also a greenhouse gas.

Microbeads Solid plastic particles of less than 1 mm in diameter that are regularly used in cosmetics and cleaning products. These are washed away down our sinks but end up back in lakes and oceans causing problems for marine life.

Microplastics Small plastic pieces or particles caused when household or industrial plastics begin to break down or disintegrate.

Natural resources Materials such as water, soil, coal and wood that are found in nature.

Nectar The sweet substance secreted by flowers and collected or eaten by insects.

Pollinate To transfer pollen to a plant or flower for fertilisation.

Preservatives Chemicals that are used to make food last longer.

Renewable energy Energy that is generated from sources like sunlight, wind or water.

Solar power The conversion of the energy from sunlight into electricity.

Sustainable Something that can be used in the present time and be replaced easily so that it can be used in the future too.

Toxin A poisonous substance.

Upcycling Reuse something and turn it into something better.

Zero waste If you want to achieve zero waste then you must make sure you reuse and recycle everything that you consume. The idea is that nothing that you use is sent to landfill.

 Find out more

Friends of the Earth
https://friendsoftheearth.uk
This international organisation is working on a global scale to help protect our world. You can join campaigns like Plastic Free Friday, Save the Bees and Campaign for Clean Air to do your bit for a greener world.

Greenpeace
www.greenpeace.org.uk
This worldwide charity has been actively involved with green causes since it was started in 1971. Today, amongst other campaigns, it is working towards stopping climate change, defending the oceans from plastic pollution, protecting rainforests, and saving the Arctic.

WaterAid
www.wateraid.org/uk/
This international organisation works around the world to supply clean water, proper toilets and sanitation and good hygiene to communities that need help.

The Freecycle Network
www.freecycle.org
The global network of community-based reuse/recycling projects. The idea is that people can give away unwanted items and acquire items they need for free.

Recycle Now
www.recyclenow.com
A UK government-backed campaign which gets behind local community recycling. As well as useful information about recycling, you can find out which recycling services are operating near you.

Gumtree
www.gumtree.com
Type in your preferred area to find items for sale or items that are being given away in your area.

Index